JB PRICE
McNair, Joseph D.
Leontyne Price / by Joseph
D. McNair.

"... the most wonderful thing in the world is to be who you are ... to be black is to shine and aim high."

—LEONTYNE PRICE

LEONTYNE PRICE

BY JOSEPH D. MCNAIR

GRAPHIC DESIGN
Robert E. Bonaker / Graphic Design & Consulting Co.

PROJECT COORDINATOR
James R. Rothaus / James R. Rothaus & Associates

EDITORIAL DIRECTION
Elizabeth Sirimarco Budd

COVER PHOTO
Leontyne Price after her last performance.
Sara Krulwich/New York Times/Archive Photos

Library of Congress Cataloging-in-Publication Data
McNair, Joseph D.
Leontyne Price / by Joseph D. McNair.
p. cm.
Includes index.
Summary: Presents a biography of the African-American opera
singer whose performance of Aida at the Metropolitan Opera
in 1961 earned her a forty-two-minute standing ovation.
ISBN 1-56766-720-1 (library : reinforced : alk. paper)

1. Price, Leontyne — Juvenile literature. 2. Sopranos (Singers)
— United States — Biography — Juvenile literature.
[1. Price, Leontyne. 2. Singers. 3. Afro-Americans —
Biography. 4. Women — Biography.] I. Title

ML3930.P745 M35 2000
782.1'092 — dc21   99-044229
[B]

Contents

Oh, What a Night!   6

The Greatest Inspiration   10

Off to School   18

A Star Is Born   25

African Prima Donna   29

A Story's End   34

Timeline   36

Glossary   37

Index   39

Further Information   40

Oh, What a Night!

"Once upon a warm, spring evening…"

The storyteller chose his words slowly, pausing between words. The group of children sitting at his feet listened closely to every word he said.

"I believe it was in the month of May. Yes, it had to be May 'cause I can smell the rosemary and honeysuckle. I can smell it growing on the mountain slopes, just like I was there. It was at the foot of Mount Zion, a hill on the eastern side of the city of Jerusalem. You children know about Mount Zion, don't you? It's in the Bible. It's a mighty special place."

Then he stopped. He let the silence fill the room. When he spoke again, his voice was barely louder than a whisper.

"Well, on that evening, in that special place, something happened. Something so special that God stopped all of the million things He was doing to pay attention."

The storyteller stared out into the darkened church basement. He looked as if he could actually see the events he described. He was a strange man, this one.

He was a huge African man with a big, deep voice. He always dressed in African clothes. He called himself Mwalimu, which means "teacher" in an African language called Kiswahili. He made his living telling stories about all kinds of people, places, and things. The stories he told best were about **African Americans.**

Sara Krulwich/New York Times Co./Archive Photos

LEONTYNE PRICE IS RECOGNIZED
AS ONE OF THE GREATEST OPERA
SINGERS OF ALL TIME.

CORBIS/Shai Ginott

In 1978, Leontyne Price sang at the foot of Mt. Zion in the city of Jerusalem. The concert was in honor of the 30th anniversary of the nation of Israel.

Mwalimu came to the church every Thursday evening without fail. He always insisted that the lights be lowered during his stories. All the children sat on the floor around him.

"You see, children, they had this big concert. It was in the country of Israel. Musicians from all over the world came to celebrate the 30th birthday of the state of Israel. Now we all know that Israel is much older than just 30 years. But the modern state of Israel was created in 1948, in what was once called **Palestine.**

"My, my, my, what a concert it was. It was outside in the open air in a town called Gehenna. This town sits in the stony valley at the foot of Mount Zion. The musicians played **classical music** that night. Nearly one hundred performers filled the stage.

"There were stars on the stage and stars in the sky. But the star who shone brightest of all was an African woman from America. This woman's singing voice was powerfully sweet.

"The **Muslims** say that in the lands around Mt. Zion, if you are quiet, you can hear the voices of dead souls crying out in the night. This woman's voice was so pure that the steady whisper of the dead stopped. It was as if everyone were holding their breath.

"The woman's name was Leontyne (LEE-un-teen) Price. And that night in Gehenna, her soul sang true.

> *He's got the whole world, in his hands*
>
> *He's got the whole wide world, in his hands*
>
> *He's got the whole world, in his hands*
>
> *He's got the whole world in his hands ...."*

Knowing that he had the children's attention, the storyteller sat back in his chair. He began to tell them the story of Leontyne's life.

The Greatest Inspiration

Katherine Bates had always dreamed of being a nurse, but things had not turned out exactly as she had hoped. She was the daughter of a preacher from Mississippi. She left her hometown to attend college. Unfortunately, money ran out before she could finish her studies. She had to drop out of college. Kate, as her family called her, moved to the town of Laurel, Mississippi. In that town, she lived with her sister and brother-in-law. Soon she was working as a **midwife.**

After a while, Kate met a carpenter named James Anthony Price. James was also the son of a preacher. The two young people had a lot in common. They fell in love and decided to get married. Together they worked hard and saved enough money to start a family.

On February 10, 1927, Mary Violet Leontine Price was born. (The family spelled "Leontine" with an "i" instead of a "y.") This event changed Kate's life forever. She never again wished she had become a nurse. In the years that followed, she became her daughter's greatest inspiration. Two years later, Leontine's brother, George, was born.

There was always music in the Prices' home. Kate was a member of the St. Paul Methodist Church choir. Everyone talked about how beautifully she sang. James was a musician, too. He played the tuba in the church band. At home, the family listened to music of all kinds.

Leontine's mother recognized that her daughter had musical talent. The young girl always sang. She could remember melodies, too. Kate decided to find a music teacher for her.

Look Magazine Photo Collection/Library of Congress

AFTER SHE BECAME A FAMOUS SINGER, LEONTYNE VISITED HER FAMILY IN LAUREL, MISSISSIPPI, WHENEVER SHE COULD. THE PRICE FAMILY ALWAYS ENCOURAGED LEONTYNE'S LOVE OF MUSIC.

Mrs. Hattie McInnis was a well-respected pianist in town. Kate asked her to teach Leontine and George to play music. For the next two-and-a-half years, Leontine's life was filled with piano lessons. She loved to practice. She enjoyed it more than playing hopscotch or jumping rope. She loved to practice even more than being with her friends. There was something inside of her that reached out to music.

Mrs. McInnis presented Leontine in her first piano **recital** when she was six years old. She did so well that her father bought a second-hand piano. The Prices did not have a lot of money. Buying a piano was a big sacrifice. But James loved his daughter, and he knew she was talented. Now Leontine had a piano of her very own.

Leontine started elementary school in 1933. Her school had an excellent music program. Kate Price made sure her daughter participated in it. Leontine played the piano or sang in most of the school's music shows. She studied dance, acting, and acrobatics as well. Even with all of this activity, Leontine was an excellent student. She got straight A's in her "letters and numbers."

Leontine knew that music would always be part of her life, but she did not know how important it would become. She had never really thought about what she might do with her talent. Then one day, in 1936, Leontine and her mother traveled to the city of Jackson, Mississippi. They were on their way to a very special event.

Leontine could see that black people and white people lived very differently in the southern United States. Many African American women cleaned houses for "white folks." Others took care of white children. Most of the men, like Leontine's father, worked at the mill or in a factory. African Americans seldom had the best jobs. Very few were preachers, lawyers, teachers, nurses, or doctors.

©CORBIS

WORKERS UNLOAD HEAVY LOGS AT A MILL IN LAUREL, MISSISSIPPI. JAMES PRICE, LIKE MANY OTHER AFRICAN AMERICANS IN LAUREL, WORKED FOR A LUMBER MILL. AS A CHILD, LEONTYNE REALIZED THAT AFRICAN AMERICANS DID NOT HAVE THE SAME OPPORTUNITIES THAT WHITE PEOPLE DID.

Leontine probably didn't imagine doing anything different with her life. Perhaps she dreamed of teaching music, just like Mrs. McInnis did. Perhaps she thought about being a midwife like her mother. Maybe she even wanted to be a nurse one day.

Kate Price had other plans for her daughter. Leontine's fate would be nothing so ordinary. She took Leontine to Jackson to give her a different vision of the future. If Leontine did not recognize her great talent, her mother certainly did.

That evening in Jackson, Leontine and her mother attended a concert. It featured Marian Anderson, one of the greatest American singers of the time.

Marian Anderson was an African American from Pennsylvania. She was born in 1897. People began to notice her beautiful voice when she was just six years old. Her church paid for voice lessons to help develop her talent. One day she was old enough to give concerts.

Anderson knew a lot about **discrimination.** People stopped her from singing on stage many times. They did this because she was black. Anderson decided to leave the United States. She planned to go to Europe to pursue her dream. Marian Anderson had to leave her own country to get the appreciation she deserved.

Anderson had just returned to the United States a few months before her concert in Jackson. She knew from experience that many public places in the South were **segregated.** That meant that black people could not sit with white people. Even worse, African Americans often were not allowed inside segregated theaters at all.

Anderson made her own plans for the Jackson concert. She refused to perform anywhere where African Americans were not treated fairly. She said the concert had to be held at a hall where all people, black or white, could attend.

AT THE PEAK OF HER CAREER, MARIAN ANDERSON WAS
ONE OF THE GREATEST SINGERS IN THE WORLD.

©Roger Ressmeyer/CORBIS

AS A CHILD, LEONTYNE NEVER IMAGINED THAT WHEN SHE GREW UP, SHE WOULD SING FOR AUDIENCES ALL AROUND THE WORLD.

That night, Marion Anderson showed Leontine how beautiful the human voice could be. Her voice was so clear and pure. She sang with confidence. She sang songs in other languages. She sang African American **spirituals** with great beauty and dignity.

Leontine felt as if she were in a trance throughout Anderson's performance. Something inside her moved. Young Leontine began to dream of a new future. That night, Leontine knew what she would be when she grew up — a singer.

IN 1939, A WHITE WOMEN'S GROUP, THE DAUGHTERS OF THE AMERICAN REVOLUTION, STOPPED MARIAN ANDERSON FROM SINGING AT CONSTITUTION HALL. THEY BELIEVED A BLACK WOMAN SHOULD NOT PERFORM IN SUCH A HISTORIC PLACE. MARIAN WOULD NOT GIVE UP. ON EASTER SUNDAY, SHE GAVE A CONCERT IN FRONT OF THE LINCOLN MEMORIAL. MARIAN REFUSED TO ACCEPT DISCRIMINATION. SHE HELPED MAKE IT POSSIBLE FOR FUTURE AFRICAN AMERICAN SINGERS TO ACHIEVE SUCCESS.

Archive Photos

Off to School

In 1937, Leontine entered the sixth grade. She attended Oak Park Vocational High School. Oak Park was a school especially for black children. It was said to be one of the best schools in Mississippi.

Mrs. McInnis taught school at Oak Park. She continued to guide Leontine's music training. She made sure that Leontine became a member of the choral group. Leontine also kept singing at St. Paul Methodist Church.

All along, Leontine's parents made plans for her to attend college. In 1944, she graduated from high school with excellent grades. She even received a **scholarship.** Leontine traveled to Ohio to attend Wilberforce University. Her plan was to become a music teacher after college.

Wilberforce University was the first **historically African American college** in the United States. It was established before the American Civil War. At the time, 30,000 African Americans lived in Ohio. Wilberforce was established to give them a chance to get an education. Before that time, it was nearly impossible for African Americans to go to college.

When Leontine left Laurel, she worried about leaving home. She knew she would miss her family. But she also knew she could not achieve her goals in the small town of Laurel. What would her life be like away from her family? Would she find a music teacher as good as Mrs. McInnis?

©Bettmann/CORBIS

LEONTYNE PRICE IS A SOPRANO. SOPRANOS HAVE
THE HIGHEST VOICES OF ALL FEMALE SINGERS.

At Wilberforce, Leontine worked with Catherine Van Buren. Mrs. Van Buren was a "voice coach." She taught singers how to use their voices to produce beautiful sound. She helped Leontine learn to sing even more beautifully.

Another important person noticed Leontine, too. His name was Charles H. Wesley, the president of Wilberforce University. Wesley heard Leontine sing in a school concert. He suggested that she change her studies from music education to voice training. He believed she could become a professional singer.

Leontine soon became the featured **soloist** in a college vocal group, the Wilberforce Singers. She was also a regular soloist in the college choir and at her church. She later transferred to Central State College and graduated with honors in 1948.

Leontine believed she still had more to learn. Where could she go to continue her education? There was only one place: the famous Juilliard School of Music in New York City.

Juilliard opened in October 1905. At the time, it was called the Institute of Musical Arts. Dr. Frank Damrosch started the school to educate students in classical music. Juilliard soon became the best music school in the country.

Kate and James Price still did not have much money, but they wanted to send Leontine to Juilliard. They worked harder than ever to help pay her **tuition.** They even took out a bank loan to help her. Leontine also worked hard. She received help from the Chisholm family from her hometown as well. Leontine's aunt and uncle worked for the Chisholms. Mr. and Mrs. Chrisholm were kind people who were happy to help the talented girl from Laurel.

The Juilliard School

DR. FRANK DAMROSCH WAS THE FOUNDER OF
JUILLIARD. HIS GOAL WAS TO ESTABLISH A MUSIC
SCHOOL THAT WOULD BE AS GOOD OR BETTER
THAN THOSE OF EUROPE. DAMROSCH WAS THE
GODSON OF A FAMOUS GERMAN COMPOSER,
FRANZ LISZT. WEALTHY AMERICAN MERCHANTS
AND BANKERS HELPED DAMROSCH FINANCE WHAT
HAS BECOME THE TOP PLACE IN AMERICA TO
STUDY MUSIC AND THE ARTS.

21

eontine also received help from a famous singer and actor, Paul Robeson. Robeson was good at almost everything he did. He was an athlete, actor, singer, scholar, and **activist.** He spoke more than 20 different languages, including several African languages. He became a famous singer. Robeson also fought fearlessly against **racism.** In 1948, Robeson heard Leontine sing in concert. He believed the world needed to hear her beautiful voice. Robeson gave a special concert. Then he donated all the money he earned to help Leontine pay for her tuition to Juilliard.

Look Magazine Photograph Collection/Library of Congress

LEONTYNE TAKES A MOMENT BEFORE A CONCERT IN HER HOMETOWN TO TALK WITH MRS. ALEXANDER CHISHOLM. THE CHISHOLM FAMILY RECOGNIZED LEONTYNE'S TALENT AND HELPED PAY HER TUITION AT JULLIARD.

©Bettmann/CORBIS

PAUL ROBESON WAS THE FIRST AFRICAN
AMERICAN ACTOR TO BECOME A TRUE MOVIE
STAR. HE BROUGHT DIGNITY AND RESPECT
TO BLACK CHARACTERS IN THE MOVIES.

Van Vechten Collection/Library of Congress

LEONTYNE IN **1951,** ONE YEAR BEFORE SHE GRADUATED FROM JUILLIARD. THE OPERA WORLD QUICKLY TOOK NOTICE OF LEONTYNE'S TALENT. SHE APPEARED IN HER FIRST PROFESSIONAL OPERA THE SAME YEAR SHE FINISHED SCHOOL.

A Star Is Born

In 1949, Leontine entered the Juilliard School of Music. It was there that she began training to become an **opera** singer. She met a well-known voice teacher, Florence Kimball. Kimball remained her teacher and friend long after Leontine left the school.

An opera is a play set to music. All the actors sing their parts instead of speaking them. The first people to do this lived a long time ago, during the **Middle Ages.** At that time, people sang and acted out stories from the Bible at church. They also sang about the Christian saints. Later, **composers** began to use other well-known stories for their operas. Eventually, opera was popular all over Europe.

Before she went to Juilliard, Leontine had only heard opera on the radio. Sometimes she listened to a Saturday afternoon radio program. It featured the famous **Metropolitan Opera Company** of New York City.

Finally, Leontine saw her first opera, *Salome* (SAH-loh-may). The opera deeply affected her. It was like the first time she heard Marian Anderson sing so many years before. More than ever, Leontine wanted to be an opera singer.

FLORENCE KIMBALL WAS A RESPECTED VOICE TEACHER AT JUILLIARD. SHE HELPED LEONTYNE IMPROVE HER VOICE AND PREPARE FOR A CAREER IN OPERA.

The Juilliard School

Leontine **auditioned** for the Juilliard Opera Workshop. It was then that the hard work of becoming an opera singer began. The words to most operas are not written in English. Leontine had to learn several new languages. She also had to learn how to act. Most important, she had to learn skills that would make her great voice even better.

Leontine appeared in a small opera role. Then she was cast in a more important part in an opera called *Falstaff*.

An American opera composer named Virgil Thompson saw Leontyne in *Falstaff*. (About this time, Leontyne began to spell her name with a "y.") Thompson wanted her to take a role in his new opera. Leontyne graduated from Juilliard in 1952. That same year, she appeared in Thompson's opera, called *Four Saints in Three Acts*. She even traveled to Paris, France, to perform the opera.

Leontyne was then cast in the lead role of another opera called *Porgy and Bess*. It was written by an American composer named George Gershwin. Leontyne's performance received **rave reviews.** She toured countries such as Austria, Germany, and France while performing in the opera.

In 1955, Marian Anderson became the first African American to sing with the Metropolitan Opera. The next year, Leontyne accomplished an important feat as well. The National Broadcasting Company (NBC) featured her in a television production of the opera *Tosca*. NBC took a huge risk by casting a black woman in the lead role. At the time, many white Americans did not like this decision. They were especially angry because her character was in love with a white man. Nonetheless, Leontyne became the first African American opera singer to appear in an opera on television.

Schomburg Collection/New York Public Library

LEONTYNE STARRED IN THE 1955 TELEVISION PRODUCTION OF *TOSCA.* THE TELEVISION PRODUCERS WERE SO IMPRESSED WITH HER TALENT THAT THEY CAST HER IN ANOTHER IMPORTANT ROLE ONE YEAR LATER. IN 1956, SHE STARRED IN *THE MAGIC FLUTE,* AN OPERA BY WOLFGANG MOZART.

Archive Photos

LEONTYNE FIRST APPEARED IN THE ROLE
OF AIDA IN 1957. SHE WOULD PERFORM
THE ROLE MANY MORE TIMES THROUGHOUT
HER CAREER.

African Prima Donna

Giuseppe Verdi was one of the greatest opera composers of all time. In 1869, he wrote *Aida* (pronounced eye-EE-dah). This opera is named after its main character, an Ethiopian girl named Aida. Verdi wrote it for the leader of Egypt to honor two important events. The first was the opening of the **Suez Canal.** The second was the opening of the Cairo Opera House. (Cairo is Egypt's capital city.)

Almost a century after Verdi composed his famous opera, Leontyne Price appeared as Aida in San Francisco. One year later, in 1959, she performed the same role at La Scala theater in Milan, Italy. La Scala is the most famous opera theater in the world. After her performance, one Italian **critic** said that Leontyne Price was "the ideal Aida." He said that even Verdi would agree if he were alive.

Leontyne has always had a special love for Aida. In 1990, she wrote a book in which she told the story of Aida. "Aida has given me inspiration on stage and off," she said.

Appearing with the Metropolitan Opera is a great honor for any singer. Being asked to perform on the first night of the opera season is even more special. On January 27, 1961, Leontyne Price performed the lead in another Verdi opera called *Il Trovatore.* (In Italian, *trovatore* means a traveling musician. It is pronounced TRO-va-TOR-eh.) She became the first African American to appear in a lead role on opening night at "The Met." At the end of her performance, another event made history. The audience gave Leontyne Price a 42-minute **standing ovation.**

Since that day, Leontyne Price has been a **prima donna,** which means "first lady" in Italian. A prima donna is the female lead, or the most important woman in an opera.

Leontyne has long been one of the most famous opera singers in the world. In 1966, she starred in the first performance at the new Lincoln Center in New York. Lincoln Center is still the largest opera house in the world. She went on to perform in theaters all over the world.

In 1985, Leontyne was ready to retire. On January 3, she gave a tearful farewell performance as Aida. She was only 57 years old. Her voice was still beautiful. Why did she decide to leave the world of opera?

The great singer told friends that she wanted to leave "standing up, like a well-mannered guest at a party." And what better way to go out than as Aida.

"Her deep devotion and love for her country and for her people — her nobility, strength, and courage — are all qualities I aspire to as a human being," she has said of Aida. Leontyne is remembered for the same reasons.

Leontyne may have stopped performing in operas, but she didn't stop singing. Today she continues to give recitals around the world. She is the **mentor** for other African American opera singers, such as Kathleen Battle, Jessye Norman, Leona Mitchell, Cynthia Clarey, and Gwendolyn Bradley.

Diva means "goddess" in Italian. Divas are the goddesses of the opera world. Leontyne Price has been called a diva. Some people believe her singing voice was the greatest of the 20th century. She has certainly won enough honors and awards to prove it.

©Bettmann/CORBIS

LEONTYNE IN COSTUME FOR HER ROLE IN
IL TROVATORE. IN 1961, LEONTYNE
BECAME THE FIRST BLACK SINGER TO
APPEAR IN A STARRING ROLE ON OPENING
NIGHT AT THE METROPOLITAN OPERA.

©Ira Nowinski/CORBIS

LEONTYNE PRICE AND FAMOUS OPERA STAR LUCIANO PAVAROTTI
PERFORM IN *AIDA*. PAVAROTTI STARRED AS RADAMES, THE
EGYPTIAN WARRIOR WHOM AIDA LOVES.

Over the years, Leontyne has won 19 Grammy Awards and three Emmy Awards. President Lyndon Johnson awarded her the 1964 Presidential Medal of Freedom. President Ronald Reagan presented her with the First Medal of Arts in 1985. Other honors include the Handel Medallion from the city of New York (1985), the Order of Merit from the Republic of Italy (1986), the French Order of Arts and Letters (1986), the Image Award from Associated Black Charities (1987), the Lifetime Achievement Award from the National Academy of Recording Arts and Sciences (1989), and the 1990 Essence Award.

Aida's Story

Aida is set in ancient Egypt. In the opera, Radames (RAH-duh-meez) is a young Egyptian warrior. He leads the Egyptian armies against Ethiopia. The armies have captured Aida, an Ethiopian girl. Aida becomes the slave of the princess of Egypt. No one knows it, but Aida is the daughter of the Ethiopian king.

Aida meets Radames, and they fall deeply in love. The Egyptian princess also loves Radames. She becomes jealous when she suspects that he loves Aida.

Radames and the Egyptian army finally defeat Ethiopia. But then Radames learns that his beloved Aida is the daughter of his enemy's king. Radames and Aida meet in secret. He vows to flee from Egypt with her.

The princess learns of their plans. She becomes jealous and tells others to capture them. Aida escapes, but Radames is caught. He is then sentenced to be buried alive in a sealed tomb.

Aida cannot live without Radames, so she secretly joins him in the tomb. Radames and Aida prepare to die together. As the opera ends, the Princess becomes ashamed of her jealousy. She prays for peace between the two warring countries.

A Story's End

The room was quiet when the storyteller finished his story. No one moved a muscle. Then the storyteller stood up. He leaned on his carved African cane. His eyes were on fire. His strong voice boomed across that church basement.

"I want you children to remember one thing. Leontyne Price came out of Mississippi — and out of the African American people. She did not come from a rich family. She had no special advantages.

"But Leontyne had a special talent. She perfected that talent until it took her to the top of her world. She is indeed our African Prima Donna, our first lady of opera. Take the talent you have, however great or small, and use it, children! You might find your way to the top of the world, too!"

©Roger Ressmeyer/CORBIS

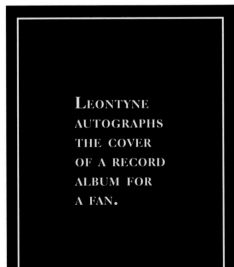

LEONTYNE AUTOGRAPHS THE COVER OF A RECORD ALBUM FOR A FAN.

©Ira Nowinski/CORBIS

Timeline

1927 Mary Violet Leontine Price is born on February 10 in Laurel, Mississippi.

1932 Leontine begins taking piano lessons with Hattie McInnis.

1933 James Price purchases a second-hand piano for Leontine.

1936 Leontine and her mother Kate attend a concert given by Marian Anderson in Jackson, Mississippi.

1937 Leontine begins classes at Oak Park Vocational High School.

1944 Leontine graduates from high school and enters Wilberforce University.

1948 Leontine graduates from Central State College. Paul Robeson hears her sing. He decides to help pay for her education at the Juilliard School of Music.

1949 Leontine wins a scholarship to Juilliard.

1952 Leontine graduates from Juilliard and begins to spell her name with a "y."

Leontyne sings *Four Saints in Three Acts*. She then sings the lead role of Bess in *Porgy and Bess*. She travels to Europe with the cast of *Porgy and Bess*.

1955 Leontyne becomes the first African American singer to perform in an opera on television.

1957 Leontyne is cast in the starring role in *Aida* for the first time.

1959 Leontyne performs the lead in *Aida* at La Scala theater in Milan, Italy. A critic describes her as "the ideal Aida."

1961 Leontyne performs the female lead on opening night of the season for New York's Metropoliton Opera. She receives a 42-minute standing ovation at the end of the performance.

1964 Leontyne is awarded the Presidential Medal of Freedom.

1978 On May 11, Leontyne performs at a concert to honor the 30th anniversary of Israel's independence.

1985 On January 3, Leontyne performs the lead in *Aida* for the last time at the Metropolitan Opera. She then retires from the world of opera.

Leontyne writes a children's book that tells the story of *Aida*.

Glossary

activist (AK-ti-vist)
An activist is a person who speaks out for what he or she believes is right. Paul Robeson was an activist.

African Americans (AF-rih-kun uh-MAYR-ih-kunz)
African Americans are black Americans whose ancestors came from Africa. Leontyne Price is an African American.

audition (awe-DISH-un)
If people audition, they give a performance for others to judge. People often audition for an important role in a play or opera, or to be accepted to a group or school.

classical music (KLAS-ih-kull MEW-zik)
Classical music is a kind of music that originated in Europe and is often played by an orchestra or by smaller groups of musicians. The Juilliard School trains students to play classical music.

composers (kum-POH-zerz)
Composers are people who write music. Giuseppe Verdi was a composer of opera.

critic (KRIH-tik)
A critic is a person who judges works of art or artistic performances. An Italian critic said that Leontyne Price was the ideal Aida.

discrimination (dis-krim-ih-NAY-shun)
Discrimination is unfair treatment of people (such as preventing them from getting jobs or going to school) simply because they are different. African Americans have suffered from discrimination by whites.

historically African American colleges (his-TOR-ik-lee AF-rih-kun uh-MAYR-ih-kan KAWL-ih-jez)
Historically African American colleges were founded to educate black Americans who were not allowed to attend schools with white students. Leontyne Price attended Wilberforce University, the country's first college for black students.

mentor (MEN-tor)
A mentor is someone who sets an example for others. Leontyne Price is a mentor to other African American opera singers.

Metropolitan Opera Company (MEH-truh-PAWL-ih-ten AH-per-eh)
The Metropolitan Opera Company is a respected organization that presents operas in New York City. Marian Anderson was the first African American to sing with the Metropolitan Opera.

Middle Ages (MID-el AY-jez)
The Middle Ages is the period of time between the years 500 to 1500. Opera probably originated during the Middle Ages.

midwife (MID-wife)
A midwife is a person, usually a woman, who helps other women give birth to their babies. Katherine Bates Price was a midwife.

Muslims (MUHZ-lemz)
Muslims believe in the religion of Islam. They are followers of the Prophet Muhammad.

Glossary

opera (AH-per-eh)
An opera is a play set to music in which the actors and actresses sing their parts. Leontyne Price was an opera singer.

Palestine (PAL-eh-styn)
Palestine is a former country that was located on the east coast of the Mediterranean Sea. It is now divided between the countries of Israel and Jordan.

prima donna (PREE-muh DON-na)
Prima donna means "first lady" in Italian. A prima donna is the female lead, or the most important woman in an opera.

racism (RAY-sih-zim)
Racism is a negative feeling or opinion about people because of their race. Racism can be committed by individuals, large groups, or even governments.

rave reviews (RAYV ree-VEWZ)
Rave reviews are very positive comments (usually in a newspaper or magazine or on television) about an artistic performance. Leontyne got rave reviews for her performance of *Aida*.

recital (ree-SY-tull)
A recital is a concert given by a musician, singer, or dancer. Music students often give recitals to show what they have learned.

scholarship (SKAHL-er-ship)
A scholarship is money awarded to a student to help pay for his or her education. Leontyne received a scholarship to attend college.

segregated (SEH-grih-gay-ted)
If something is segregated, it cannot be used equally by all people. Many places in the South were once segregated, so African Americans either could not enter or were separated from white people.

soloist (SOH-loh-ist)
A soloist is a person who sings or plays a piece of music alone. Leontyne was a soloist at Wilberforce University concerts.

spirituals (SPEER-ih-chewlz)
Spirtuals are religious songs based on stories from the Bible. They were created and sung by African Americans, especially during the time of slavery.

standing ovation (STAN-ding oh-VAY-shun)
A standing ovation is when an audience expresses their enthusiasm for a performance by standing up, clapping their hands, and cheering. In 1962, Leontyne received a 42-minute standing ovation.

Suez Canal (SOO-ez kah-NAL)
The Suez Canal is a long, thin, man-made stretch of water that spans more than 100 miles (161 kilometers) in northeast Egypt. Composer Giuseppe Verdi wrote *Aida* in honor of the opening of the Suez Canal.

tuition (too-IH-shen)
Tuition is a fee for attending a school. A famous singer named Paul Robeson gave a concert to help pay for Leontyne's tuition.

Index

Aida
    composition of, 29
    Price's admiration for, 30
    Price's book about, 29
    story of, 33
Anderson, Marian, 14, 15, 17, 26

Bates, George, 10, 12
Bates, Kathleen, 10, 11,
    and plans for Leontyne, 14
    occupation of, 10

Central State College, 20
Chisholm family, 20, 22
classical music, 9
colleges, African American, 18

Damrosch, Frank, 20, 21
discrimination, 14
diva, 30

Egypt, 29

Israel, 6, 8, 9

Julliard School of Music, 20, 21, 24, 25-26

Kimball, Florence, 25

La Scala, 29
Lincoln Center, 30

McInnis, Hattie, 12, 14, 18
Metropolitan Opera Company, 25, 26, 29, 31
    first black singer to perform with, 26
Muslim, 9

National Broadcasting Company, 26

Oak Park High School, 18
opera, 25-26, 27, 28, 29-30, 31
    definition of, 25

Price, James Anthony, 10, 11
    occupation of, 13
    and purchase of piano, 12
Price, Leontyne (Leontine)
    awards won by, 33
    education of, 12, 18, 20, 25-26
    farewell performance of, 30, 32
    first music lessons, 10-11
and Julliard School of Music, 20, 22, 24, 25-26
    and Marian Anderson concert, 14, 17
    performances
        Aida, 28, 29-30, 32
        Falstaff, 26
        Four Saints in Three Acts, 26
        in Gehenna, 6, 8, 9
        Il Trovatore, 29, 31
        The Magic Flute, 27
        Porgy and Bess, 26
        Tosca (NBC), 26, 27
prima donna, 30, 34

rave reviews, 29
Robeson, Paul, 22, 23

St. Paul Methodist Church, 10, 18
Salome, 25
scholarship, 18
segregation, 14
soprano, 19
standing ovation, 29
Suez Canal, 29

Van Buren, Catherine, 20
Verdi, Giuseppe, 29

Wesley, Charles, 20
Wilberforce University, 18, 20

Further Information

Books

Price, Leontyne. *Aida.* New York: Harcourt Brace, 1990.

Rosenberg, J. *Sing Me a Song.* London: Thames & Hudson, 1996.

Taverna, Alessandra. *Opera.* Hauppauge, NY: Barron's, 1999.

Web Sites

To hear Leontyne Price sing:
http://www.geocities.com/Paris/Cafe/4057/operamain.html

To learn more about the opera *Aida:*
http://www.uk.sis.gov.eg/aida/html/story.htm

To learn more about Leontyne Price:
http://Kennedy-center.org/honors/years/price.html

http://www.afrovoices.com/price.html

http:/wipux1.wifo.uni-mannheim.de/~bw102392/wunderlich/bios/price.htm

To visit the homepage of the Metropolitan Opera:
http://www.metopera.org/metopera.html